American Cookery

American Cookery:

OR, THE ART OF DRESSING

Viands, Fish, Poultry and Vegetables,

AND THE BEST MODES OF MAKING

Puff-Pastes, Pies, Tarts, Puddings, Custards and Preserves,

AND ALL KINDS OF

C A K E S,

From the Imperial PLUMB to plain CAKE.

ADAPTED TO THIS COUNTRY,

AND ALL GRADES OF LIFE.

BY A M E L I A S I M M O N S,
AN AMERICAN ORPHAN.

A BICENTENNIAL FACSIMILE
OF THE SECOND EDITION, ALBANY [1796]

WITH AN INTRODUCTION BY
K A R E N H E S S

APPLEWOOD BOOKS
BEDFORD, MASSACHUSETTS

The second edition of *American Cookery* was first published in 1796 in Albany, New York. It was published by Charles R. and George Webster.

ISBN 13: 978-1-55709-439-1

Thank you for purchasing an Applewood Book. Applewood reprints America's lively classics—books from the past that are of interest to modern readers. For a free copy of our current catalog, write to: Applewood Books, P.O. Box 365, Bedford, MA 01730.

Applewood Books would like to thank Karen Hess for her help in bringing this edition to our attention and for her patient insistence that it be published in facsimile. Historical notes copyright © 1996 by Karen Hess.
The original copy of the 1796 edition from which this facsimile was produced is in the collections of the Rare Books and Manuscripts Division, Center for the Humanities, the New York Public Library. Used by permission of The New York Public Library, Astor, Lenox and Tilden Foundations.

Printed in the United States of America.

Library of Congress Cataloging-in-Publication Data
Simmons, Amelia.
      American cookery, or, The art of dressing viands, fish, poultry and vegetables, and the best modes of making puff-pastes, pies, tarts, puddings, custards and preserves, and all kinds of cakes; from the imperial plumb to plain cake, adapted to this country, and all grades of life / by Amelia Simmons; with an introduction by Karen Hess.
      p.   cm.
      Reprint of 2nd ed. Originally published: Albany, N.Y.: C.R. Webster, 1796.
      ISBN 13: 978-1-55709-439-1
      1. Cookery, American—Early works to 1800.   I. Title.
TX703.S5   1996
641.5973–dc20   96-13323
                                                    CIP

TABLE OF CONTENTS

(v)

ACKNOWLEDGEMENTS

First, I want to pay tribute to the pioneering contributions in the study of American culinary history by Mary Tolford Wilson, author of *The First American Cookbook*, an essay that served as the introduction to the beautiful facsimile of the first edition of *American Cookery* by Amelia Simmons, 1796, published by Oxford University Press in 1958, a landmark work. I have often had occasion to cite her work, and in the present case, it is primordial. Indeed, for anyone with more than a casual interest in culinary Americana, it is required reading. (I note that Dover has re-issued the Oxford edition.)

I also want to acknowledge the contributions of my friend, the late Eleanor Lowenstein, whose *Bibliography of American Cookery Books 1742-1860* is the bible of all workers in culinary Americana in this regard. It was she who painstakingly established the correct date of the original publication of the second edition of *American Cookery*, citing an advertisement in the *Albany Gazette*, October 31, 1796. And yes, it is the same date as that of the first edition, 1796, so this truly is a bicentennial year for American cookbooks.

I cannot write on culinary history without acknowledging my debt to my friend and mentor, the late Elizabeth David. I should also mention Jan Longone, bibliographer and bookseller, and Joe Carlin, bookseller, who have aided and abetted me often in the past and specifically in this particular project.

This bicentennial year should have occasioned a serious critical work with proper scholarly apparatus, but the cruel constraints of time and space prevented that. I note that the above is in lieu of certain more formal citations; for the most part, I rest on my findings in the texts themselves, occasionally differing in my conclusions with those of other historians, and on my own past works.

I want to thank the New York Public Library for having made the second edition available to me for study, now many years ago, both in the original and in photocopy.

And finally, I want to thank Applewood Books for bringing out this rare edition of what appears to be our earliest truly American cookbook author. I am particularly grateful that I was able to convince them to print it the way Amelia Simmons knew it, that is, in facsimile, rather than in a modernized form.

—Karen Hess

Other books by Karen Hess

The Taste of America. Co-author with John L. Hess. Viking, 1977; University of South Carolina Press, 1989.

English Bread and Yeast Cookery by Elizabeth David. Editor of American edition, Viking Press, 1980.

Martha Washington's Booke of Cookery. Columbia University Press, 1981.

The Virginia House-wife by Mary Randolph, 1824. Editor of facsimile edition. University of South Carolina Press, 1984.

The Carolina Rice Kitchen: The African Connection. University of South Carolina Press, 1992.

What Mrs. Fisher Knows About Old Southern Cooking by Abby Fisher, 1881. Afterword for facsimile edition, Applewood Books, 1995.

THE FIRST AMERICAN COOKBOOK, SECOND EDITION, ALBANY [1796]

Historical Notes on the Work and its Author, Amelia Simmons, An American Orphan

By Karen Hess

Cookbook publishing history in what came to be the United States of America opened in 1742 with the publication of *The Compleat Housewife* by E[liza] Smith in Williamsburg, Virginia, appropriating the fifth London edition of a work first published in 1727, known to have been in circulation in the Colonies. Indeed, English cookbooks had long been in documented use by the Colonists, going back at least to *The English Hus-wife* of 1615 by Gervase Markham. And *The Art of Cookery* by Hannah Glasse, first published in London in 1747, was far and away the most popular and influential cookbook of the late Colonial period, far surpassing those London works appearing in American editions during that period. Not one of them included specifically American recipes, although by that time a few native American products had become adopted in English cookery, beginning with turkey and so-called French beans, but gradually also both sweet and white potatoes, even chocolate, vanilla, and tomatoes, and so came to be called for in English cookbooks well before the end of the eighteenth century. But we find not one cookbook written by an American, for Americans, that is, until 1796, when *American Cookery* appeared in Hartford, and later the same year, in Albany.

Amelia Simmons changed all that. As she wrote on the title page, her work was "Adapted to this country, and all grades of life." It is not that it was otherwise strikingly original, for it was not. What it did, from a historical point of view, was to demonstrate the continuity of English culinary tradition and how it was "Adapted to this Country." And therein lies the larger story.

Who was Amelia Simmons? All we really know is that she proclaimed herself to be "An American Orphan." All else is by inference only. She speaks, a bit enviously perhaps, of "those females who have parents, or brothers, or riches," and how female orphans may be "reduced to the necessity of going into families in the line of domestics," from which it seems reasonable to conjecture that she was unmarried and had to earn her living, most likely as a servant cook in a fairly ordinary household. She claims that the "egregious blunders and inaccuracies [in the first edition]...were occasioned either by the ignorance, or evil intention of the transcriber for the press," from which we may infer that she was all but illiterate. It has been objected that the preface to both first and second editions were written by an educated person, which is true, but the recipes were not. All the more credit to Amelia Simmons for her perseverance. And, she knew that she was on to something, something important, *American Cookery*.

Let me say here that Amelia Simmons was a good cook, what we used to call a "good plain cook." Note the generous use and variety of herbs in her cooking, just for example, something we like to think we moderns invented. Or the use of wine. Or the extraordinarily fine roasting techniques, English techniques that were admired even by the French. No grey sodden roasts for Amelia Simmons. To be sure, most of us can no longer roast at the hearth, more's the pity, but we can emulate her roasting times, which are admirable. And she often makes keen culinary points that somehow all too often escape the more "sophisticated" writers of today.

And where did she hail from? Because the first edition is from Hartford, historians have always assumed that she was a New Englander. I am not so sure. Indeed, a case can be made for her being from the Hudson River valley: the second edition, 1796, is from Albany; the third, 1804, is from Salem [New York] and Albany; the 1808 edition is from Troy; the 1815 edition is from Poughkeepsie; and the 1822 edition is from New York. It is to be remarked that they are all on the Hudson River, or near it, a cluster. The other known editions are strewn about New England with no clear pattern. (I am not going to go into tedious detail over the differences among the various editions, nor how she attempted to "correct" the errors of the first edition, except to note that there are indeed many changes from that edition, including many added recipes.)

The presence in her work of a number of Dutch words lends further support to my maverick notion that perhaps we should look to the Hudson River valley rather than to Connecticut for possible traces of her existence. Chief among these words are *slaw*, from *sla*, meaning salad, and *cookey*, from *koekje*, meaning, well, cookie. In England, the word for the latter was *small cake*. In addition, hers seems to be the first American work to call for the use of potash, or as she called it, *pearl ash*, in baking. There was a particularly active production of potash in the Albany area in late Colonial times.

A digression. It is one of my laws of culinary history that print lags behind practice; the only question is by how much in any given instance. This work calls for alkali seven times, showing that it must already have been in long use, at least in her part of the country. That is, first finding does not necessarily indicate first use, indeed, rarely ever does. Nor was the practice of American origin; it had been used in England, where it was regarded as an adulterant, by mid-eighteenth century, and far earlier by the Arabs in the form of *natron*, but that is another story.

In any event, like Janus, a cookbook looks both backward and forward; while it records culinary practice in a given time and place, if a bit idiosyncratically, it also influences the cookery for decades to come in ever widening circles. In that sense, *American Cookery* could be called a book of Hudson River Valley cookery; it could also be called *New-England Cookery*, which is precisely what Lucy Emerson did with her plagiarized Montpelier edition of 1808. What it could not be called is a book of Southern American cookery. Our South was another world, where African women were stirring the pots in the slaveowner's kitchen, creating a new magical cuisine that shared certain historical origins with that of Hartford and Albany, to be sure, but was transmuted into something else by the African presence. I have had occasion to write about that phenomenon many times, but it is not part of this story.

Let us examine what some describe as uniquely American aspects of her work. It has often been claimed that her work is the first ever to call for the use of maize, or what the Colonists called *Indian corn*, often simply *indian*. Not so. Antoine Augustin Parmentier devoted an entire chapter to it in *Le Parfait Boulanger*, 1778, and he claims that a paper had previously been given on its use in making bread for the *Société Royale* at Metz, and that it had long been made in the Bearn. What is little appreciated is that the use of maize as a staple had very early spread like wildfire in the poorer parts of the world, all but displacing earlier millets and chestnuts in various breads and porridges — *mealies, polenta, mammaliga*, etc.

I have often written that the ease of adoption by a people of a new product depends on the ease with which it can be substituted for a familiar one in traditional recipes. That is, it is the kitchen use that determines this adoption, not scientific relationships, not place of origin, so that neither turkey nor American beans caused a moment's hesitation. The substitution of native American maize for oats in English recipes posed little problem, both being rather fatty grains with no gluten. This can be seen in Miss Simmons' famous *Johny Cakes*, which are not American, at least not in name, at least not originally. (It is true that her recipes seem to be the earliest in print for them, at least those made of cornmeal, but we know that they had been made in the Colonies very nearly from the beginning — not to mention the *pone* of the Native Americans — an illuminating example of the lag of the printed word.) The name comes from *jannock*, a word from northern England, especially Lancashire, referring to "oaten bread," and I maintain that *johnny cake* comes from the diminutive form, *jonikin*, being a small hearth bread. (Actually, *jannock* and *bannock*, going back to Latin *panis*, are the same word, as will be realized on reflection.) In Australia *johnny cake* refers to a wheaten flat bread, and in parts of our own South it historically more often than not referred to rice cakes. That is, *johnny cake* has little to do with maize but everything to do with the available grain, as well as the available means of baking, to be sure. Her recipes for "Indian Pudding" again refer simply to the substitution of *indian* for oatmeal in traditional English recipes.)

A word on her famous "Election Cake," one of many recipes which did not appear until the Albany edition, so that it cannot be identified specifically with Hartford, which it often is. It is simply one of the "Great Cakes" of English culinary tradition, to be made for festival occasions, huge loaves of highly enriched yeasted bread, flavored with sugar, spices, and lovely rosewater or spirits of some kind, as well as raisins or the like, recipes for which abounded in cookbooks of the seventeenth and eighteenth centuries. Certainly in 1796, Election Day would have been a major festival, a cause for celebration. The same may be said for "Independence Cake."

While we are on cakes, I might mention her gingerbreads, seven, some of which are for a softer fluffier type than earlier crisp versions, that is, of the *gingerbread man* type. The historical substitution of cheaper molasses for honey, a change that had already long been under way, and the use of alkalis to counter the acidic content of molasses, a practice that may have come from Germany, inevitably came to be used to bring about a leavening effect. Rather surprisingly, only one of these recipes calls for molasses; the others call for sugar or even honey, as in "Honey Cake." Also, while we are on cakes, I note her drying of flour in the oven before use; this was considered fine practice and, indeed, still is. Still on baking, her use of the word *shortning* was not new, as has been thought; to *shorten* doughs by adding butter or lard is documented in culinary manuscripts of the fourteenth century. Dictionaries, even august ones, are notoriously slack on the question of culinary citations.

Even her *Pompkin* pies, which she calls *puddings*, were not new. Hannah Woolley gave a recipe back in the seventeenth century; I also have Tudor recipes for custardy puddings, baked in a crust or not, based on starchy sweet roots such as parsnips or carrots, little different from the recipe for "Carrot Pudding" given by Amelia Simmons. For that matter, pumpkins are not uniquely American, although the precise variety probably was; botanists are not in agreement on *Cucurbita Pepo*. But the use of edible gourds has been documented at least as far back as ancient Rome, and there are recipes in French medieval culinary manuscripts involving forms of *citrouille, potiron, courge*, and in English ones, *gourd*. In any event, she uses English methods in all cases.

And yes, even the use of cranberries with turkey has its English precedents: the use of sweetened barberries, also red, acidy, and hard, with roasted game goes back at least to early Tudor times, in obvious imitation of the Arab use of pomegranates to garnish meats. In the *Forme of Cury*, a royal manuscript of the late fourteenth century, there is a recipe for "*Sawse Sarzyne*," based on rose hips, red wine, the red intensified with the dye *alkenet*, all to be garnished with *pomme garnet* [pomegranate]. That is, the use of sour-sweet red relishes is very ancient.

So, again, what makes *American Cookery* so very American? It is precisely the bringing together of certain native American products and English culinary traditions. So English that entire chapters were "borrowed" from *The Frugal Housewife* by Susannah Carter, which appeared in American editions in 1772 and 1792, and yet so very American in her use of those elements. By 1831, *American Cookery* had long been superseded by American editions of *A New System of Domestic Cookery* by Maria Rundell, and *The Virginia House-wife, 1824*, by our own Mary Randolph, they in turn to be doomed by the coming Industrial Revolution.

In closing, I quote Mary Tolford Wilson: "But Amelia Simmons still holds her place as the mother of American cookery books. And no later work, however completely it may reflect the mores of this country, has quite the freshness of this first glimpse caught in the small mirror held up by an American Orphan."

American Cookery :

OR, THE ART OF DRESSING
Viands, Fiſh, Poultry and Vegetables,

AND THE BEST MODES OF MAKING

Puff-Paſtes, Pies, Tarts, Puddings,
Cuſtards and Preſerves,

AND ALL KINDS OF

C A K E S,

From the Imperial PLUMB to plain CAKE.

ADAPTED TO THIS COUNTRY,

AND ALL GRADES OF LIFE.

By A M E L I A S I M M O N S,

AN AMERICAN ORPHAN.

THE SECOND EDITION.
PUBLISHED ACCORDING TO ACT OF CONGRESS.

A L B A N Y :
Printed by CHARLES R. & GEORGE WEBSTER,
*At their Printing-Office and Bookſtore, in the White-Houſe,
Corner of State and Pearl-Streets ;*

FOR THE AUTHORESS.

PREFACE.

§§*§*§*§*

AS this treatife is calculated for the im-
provement of the rifing generation of
Females in America, the Lady of fafhion
and fortune will not be difpleafed, if many hints are fuggefted for the more general and univerfal knowledge of thofe females in this country, who by the lofs of
their parents, or other unfortunate cir-
cumftances, are reduced to the neceffity
of going into families in the line of domef-
tics, or taking refuge with their friends or
relations, and doing thofe things which are
really effential to the perfecting them as
good wives, and ufeful members to focie-
ty. The orphan, tho' left to the care of
virtuous guardians, will find it effentially
neceffary to have an opinion and determination of her own. The world, and the
fafhion thereof, is fo variable, that old
people can not accommodate themfelves to
the various changes and fafhions which
daily occur ; *they* will adhere to the fafhion of *their* day, and will not furrender
their attachments to the *good old way*—
while the young and the gay, bend and
conform readily to the tafte of the times,
and fancy of the hour. By having an o-
pinion and determination, I would not be

underſtood to mean an obſtinate perſever-
ance in trifles, which borders on obſtinacy
—by no means, but only an adherence to
thoſe rules and maxims which have ſtood
the teſt of ages, and will forever eſtabliſh
the *female character*, a virtuous character
—altho' they conform to the ruling taſte
of the age in cookery, dreſs, language,
manners, &c.

It muſt ever remain a check upon the
poor ſolitary orphan, that while thoſe females that have parents, or brothers, or
riches to defend their indiſcretions, that
the orphan muſt depend ſolely upon *character*. How immenſely important, there-
fore, that every action, every word, every
thought, be regulated by the ſtricteſt pu-
rity, and that every movement meet the
approbation of the good and wiſe.

The candor of the American Ladies is ſo-
licitouſly intreated by the Authoreſs, as
ſhe is circumſcribed in her knowledge, this
being an original work in this country.
Should any future editions appear, ſhe
hopes to render it more valuable.

PREFACE TO THE SECOND EDITION.

THE Authorefs of the American Cookery, feels herfelf under peculiar obligations, publicly to acknowledge the kind patronage of fo many refpectable characters, in her attempts, to improve the minds of her own fex, and others in a line of bufinefs, which is not only neceffary ; but applies from day to day.

Notwithftanding the great difadvantages, with which, the firft edition of this work made its appearance in the world ; yet the call has been fo great, and the fale fo rapid, that fhe finds herfelf not only encouraged, but under a neceffity of publifhing a fecond edition, to accommodate a large and extenfive circle of reputable characters, who wifh to countenance the exertions of an orphan, in that which is defigned for general utility to all ranks of people in this Republic. She hopes that this fecond edition, will appear, in a great meafure, free from thofe egregious blunders, and inaccuracies, which attended the firft : which were occafioned either by the ignorance, or evil intention of the tranfcriber for the prefs.

Nearly the whole of 17 pages in the firft edition, was filled with rules, and directions, how to make choice of meats, fowls, fish, and vegetables : this is a matter, with which, the Authoress does not pretend to be acquainted, much lefs to give directions to others ; nor does fhe confider any way connected, with that branch which fhe has undertaken, which is, fimply to point out the moft eligible methods of preparing thofe various articles for the tables when procured. This was done by the tranfcriber, without her knowledge or confent ; and may with propriety be confidered as an affront upon the good fenfe of all claffes of citizens.

Long experience has abundantly taught thofe who refide in cities, and in the country, how to diftinguifh between good and bad, as to every article brought into market. This part of the former edition, fhe confidered altogether unneceffary, and accordingly has excluded it a place in this.

Many of the receipts were very erroneous, which fhe has endeavored to correct with the greateft care.

She has alfo taken pains to make confiderable additions to this work, refpecting many important articles, which were omitted in the former edition. Neither pains, nor labor have been fpared, in her feeble exertions to render this fmall tract, more acceptable, and more extenfively ufeful than the former.

Undoubtedly objections will be made and exceptions taken to many things in this work. In every inftance where this may be the cafe, fhe has only to requeft, that they would remember, that it is the performance of, and effected under all thofe difadvantages, which ufually attend, an Orphan.

RECEIPTS.

To Roaſt Beef.

THE general rules are, to have a briſk hot fire, to be placed on a ſpit, to baſte with ſalt and water, and one quarter of an hour to every pound of beef, tho' tender beef will require leſs, while old tough beef will require more roaſting; pricking with a fork will determine you whether done or not; rare done is the healthieſt, and the taſte of this age.

Roaſt Mutton.

If a breaſt let it be cauled, if a leg, ſtuffed or not, let it be done more gently than beef, and done more; the chine, ſaddle or leg require more fire and longer time than the breaſt, &c. Serve with potatoes, beans or boiled onion, caper ſauce, maſhed turnip, or lettuce.

Roaſt Veal.

As it is more tender than beef or mutton, and eaſily ſcorched, paper it, eſpecially the fat parts, let there be a briſk fire, baſte it well; a loin weighing 15lb. requires two hours and a half roaſting; garniſh with green-parſley and ſliced lemon.

Roaſt Lamb.

Lay down to a clear good fire that will not want ſtirring or altering, baſte with butter, duſt on flour, and before you take it up, add more butter and ſprinkle on a

little falt and parfley fhred fine; fend to
table with an elegant fallad, green peas,
frefh beans, or afparagus.

To alamode a round of Beef.

To a 14 or 16 pound round of beef, put
one ounce falt-petre, 48 hours after ftuff it
with the following : one and half pound
beef, half a pound falt pork, two pound
grated bread, chop all fine and rub in half
pound butter, falt pepper and cayenne,
fummer favory, thyme ; lay it on fcewers
in a large pot, over 3 pints hot water (which
it muft occafionally be fupplied with,) the
fteam of which in 4 or 5 hours will render
the round tender if over a moderate fire ;
when tender, take away the gravy and
thicken with flour and butter, and boil—
brown the round with butter and flour, adding ketchup and wine to your tafte.

To alamode a round.

Take fat pork half a pound cut in flices
or mince, feafon it with pepper, falt, fweet
marjoram and thyme, cloves and mace—
make large incifions in the beef, and ftuff
it the night before cooked ; put fome bones
acrofs the bottom of the pot to keep from
burning, put in one quart claret wine and
three pints water ; lay the round on the
bones and cover clofe ; hang on in the
morning and ftew gently three hours ;—
fcum the gravy and ferve in a butter boat,

ferve it with the refidue of the gravy in the difh.

To broil a Beef-Stake.

Take flices of tender beef one inch thick, put on hot coals 15 minutes; turn the ftake if poffible without introducing a fork; pepper and falt as may be agreeable : butter when done will render it palatable.

To drefs a Beef-Stake, fufficient for two Gentlemen, with a fire made of two newfpapers.

Let the beef be cut in flices, and laid in a pewter platter, pour on water juft fufficient to cover them, falt and pepper well cover with another platter inverted; then place your difh upon a ftool bottom upwards, the legs of fuch length as to raife the platter three inches from the board; cut your newfpapers into fmall ftrips, light with a candle and apply them gradually, fo as to keep a live fire under the whole difh, till the whole are expended when the ftake will be done; butter may then be applied, fo as to render it grateful.

Veal Stake.

Take flices of veal half an inch thick, broil 20 minutes with a live fire, falt and pepper, duft on flour when broiling; when done butter added will make a beautiful gravy.

To ftuff a Leg of Veal.

Take one pound of veal, half pound of

pork (falted,) one pound grated bread—
chop all very fine, with a handful of green
parfley, pepper it, add 3 ounces butter and
3 eggs, (and fweet herbs if you like them,)
make large incifions in the leg, and fill in
all the ftuffing; then falt and pepper the
leg and duft on fome flour; if baked in
an oven, put into a fauce pan with a little
water, if potted, lay fome fcewers at the
bottom of the pot, put in a little water and
lay the leg on the fcewers with a gentle
fire to render it tender, (frequently adding
water,) when done take out the leg, put
butter in the pot and brown the leg, the
gravy in a feparate veffel muft be thicken-
ed and buttered, a fpoonful of ketchup added, and wine if agreeable.

To ftuff a Pig, to roaft or bake.

Boil the inwards tender, mince fine, add
half loaf bread, half pound butter, 4 eggs,
falt, pepper, fweet marjorum, fage, fummer
favory, thyme, mix the whole well together; ftuff and few up: If the pig be large
let it be doing two and a half hours; bafte
with falt and water.

Gravy for the fame. Half pound butter,
work in two fpoons flour, one gill water, one
gill wine if agreeable.

To ftuff a leg of Pork to bake or roaft.

Corn the leg 48 hours and ftuff with fau-
fage meat and bake in a hot oven 2 hours
and an half or roaft.

To stuff a Turkey.

Grate a wheat loaf, 1 quarter of a pound butter, one quarter of a pound salt pork, finely chopped, 2 eggs, a little sweet marjoram, summer-savory, parsley, pepper and salt (if the pork be not sufficient,) fill the bird and sew up.

The same will answer for all Wild Fowl. *Water Fowls* require onions.

The same ingredients stuff a *leg of Veal*, *fresh Pork* or a *loin of Veal*.

To stuff and roast a Turkey or Fowl.

One pound soft wheat bread, 3 ounces beef suet, 3 eggs, a little sweet thyme, sweet marjoram, pepper and salt, and some add a gill of wine ; fill the bird therewith and sew up, hang down to a steady solid fire, basting frequently with butter and water, and roast until a steam emits from the breast, put one third of a pound of butter into the gravy, dust flour over the bird and baste with the gravy ; serve up with boiled onions and cramberry-sauce, mangoes, pickles or celery.

2. Others omit the sweet herbs, and add parsley done with potatoes.

3. Boil and mash 3 pints potatoes, moisten them with butter, add sweet herbs, pepper, salt, fill and roast as above.

To stuff and roast a Goslin,

Boil the inwards tender, chop them fine,

put double quantity of grated bread, four ounces butter, pepper, falt, (and fweet herbs if you like) and 2 eggs into the ftuffing, add wine, and roaft the bird.

The above is a good ftuffing for every kind of Water Fowl, which requires onion fauce.

To ftuff and roaft four Chickens.

Six ounces falt pork, half loaf bread, fix ounces butter, 3 eggs, a handful of parfley fhreded fine, fummer-favory, fweet marjoram ; mix the whole well together, fill and few up ; roaft one hour, bafte with butter, and duft on flour.

Gravy for the fame. Half pint water, half pound butter, 3 fpoons flour, a little falt, and wine if you like.

The fame compofition will anfwer for *fix* PIGEONS, roafted in the pot. The pigeons muft be kept from burning by laying fcewers on the bottom of the pot, adding three pints water ; cover clofe, let them do one hour and a quarter ; when done pour on one quart ftewed oyfters, well feafoned with butter and pepper.

To broil Chickens.

Take thofe which are young and tender, break the breaft bone, feafon high with pepper and falt, broil half an hour on hot coals. Six ounces butter, 3 fpoons water, and a little flour will make a gravy.

PIGEONS may be broiled in the fame way in twenty minutes.

To fmother a Fowl in Oyfters.

Gill the bird with dry oyfters, and few up and boil in water juft fufficient to cover the bird, falt and feafon to your tafte—when done tender, put it into a deep difh and pour over it a pint of ftewed oyfters, well buttered and peppered, garnifh a turkey with fprigs of parfley or leaves of cellery : a fowl is beft with a parfley fauce.

To drefs a Turtle.

Fill a boiler or kettle, with a quantity of water fufficient to fcald the callapach and callapee, the fins, &c. and about 9 o'clock hang up your turtle by the hind fins, cut of the head and fave the blood, take a fharp pointed knife and feparate the callapach from the callapee, or the back from the belly part, down to the fhoulders, fo as to come at the entrails which take out, and clean them, as you would thofe of any other animal, and throw them into a tub of clean water, taking great care not to break the gall, but to cut it off from the liver and throw it away, then feparate each diftinctly and put the guts into another veffel, open them with a fmall pen-knife end to end, wafh them clean, and draw them through a woolen cloth, in warm water, to clear away the flime and then put them in

clean cold water till they are ufed with the
other part of the entrails, which muft be
cut up fmall to be mixed in the baking
difhes with the meat ; this done feparate
the back and belly pieces, entirely cutting
away the fore fins by the upper joint, which
fcald ; peal off the loofe fkin and cut them
into fmall pieces, laying them by themfelves, either in another veffel, or on the table, ready to be feafoned ; then cut off the
meat from the belly part and clean the
back from the lungs, kidneys, &c. and
that meat cut into pieces as fmall as a wal-
nut, laying it likewife by itfelf; after this,
you are to fcald the back and belly pieces,
pulling off the fhell from the back, and the
yellow fkin from the belly, when all will
be white and clean, and with the kitchen
cleaver cut thofe up likewife into pieces a-
bout the bignefs or breadth of a card ;——
put thofe pieces into clean cold water, wafh
them and place them in a heap on the table, fo that each part may lay by itfelf ;
the meat being thus prepared and laid feparate for feafoning ; mix two thirds of falt
or rather more, and one third part of cayenne pepper, black pepper, and a nutmeg,
and mace pounded fine, and mixt all together ; the quantity to be proportioned
to the fize of the turtle, fo that in each
difh there may be about three fpoonfuls of

feafoning to every twelve pound of meat;
your meat being thus feafoned, get fome
fweet herbs, fuch as thyme, favory, &c. let
them be dried and rubb'd fine, and having
provided fome deep difhes to bake it in,
which fhould be of the common brown
ware, put in the coarfeft part of the meat,
put a quarter pound of butter at the bottom of each difh—and then put fome of
each of the feveral parcels of meat, fo that
the difhes may be all alike and have equal
pofitions of the different parts of the turtle,
and between each laying of meat ftrew a
little of the mixture of fweet herbs, fill your
difhes within an inch and an half, or two
inches of the top; boil the blood of the
turtle, and put into it, then lay on forced
meat balls, made of veal, highly feafoned
with the fame feafoning as the turtle; put
in each difh a gill of Madeira wine, and
as much water as it will conveniently hold,
then break over it five or fix eggs to keep
the meat from fcorching at the tcp, and o-
ver that fhake a handful of fhred parfley,
to make it look green, when done put your
difhes into an oven made hot enough to
bake bread, and in an hour and half, or
two hours (according to the fize of the difhes) it will be fufficiently done.

To drefs a Calve's Head. Turtle fafhion.

The head and feet being well fcalded

and cleaned, open the head, taking the brains, wafh, pick and cleanfe, falt and pepper and parfley them and put by in a cloth; boil the head, feet and heartflet one and quarter, or one and half hour, fever out the bones, cut the fkin and meat in flices, ftrain the liquor in which boiled and put by; clean the pot very clean or it will burn too, make a layer of the flices, which duft with a compofition made of black pepper, one fpoon of fweet herbs pulverized, two fpoons (fweet marjoram and thyme are moft approved) a tea fpoon of cayenne, one pound butter, then duft with flour, then a layer of flices with flices of veal and feafoning till completed, cover with the liquor, ftew gently three quarters of an hour. To make the forced meat balls— take one and a half pound veal, one pound grated bread, four ounces raw falt pork— mince and feafon with above, and work with 3 whites into balls, one or one an half inch diameter, roll in flour, and fry in very hot butter till brown, then chop the brains fine and ftir into the whole mefs in the pot, put thereto, one third part of the fried balls and a pint of wine or lefs, when all is heated thro' take off, and ferve in tureens, laying the refidue of the balls and hard boiled and pealed eggs into a difh, garnifh with flices of lemon.

Alamode Beef.

Take a round of beef, and ſtuff it with half pound pork, half pound of butter, the ſoft of half a loaf of wheat bread, boil four eggs very hard, chop them up ; add ſweet marjoram, ſage, parſley, ſummerſavory, and one ounce of cloves pounded, chop them all together, with two eggs very fine, and add a gill of wine, ſeaſon very high with ſalt and pepper, cut holes in your beef, to put your ſtuffing in, then ſtick whole cloves into the beef, then put it into a two pail pot, with ſticks at the bottom, if you wiſh to have the beef round when done, put it into a cloth and bind it tight with 20 or 30 yards of twine, put it into your pot with two or three quarts of water, and one gill of wine, if the round be large it will take three or four hours to bake it.

Soup, made of a beef's hock.

Let the bones be well broken, boil five hours in eight quarts water, one gill rice to be added, ſalt ſufficiently ; after three hours boiling add 12 potatoes pared, ſome ſmall carrots and two onions ; a little ſummerſavory will make it grateful,

Veal Soup.

Take a ſhoulder of veal, boil in five quarts water three hours, with two ſpoons rice, four onions, ſix potatoes, and a few carrots, ſweet marjorum, parſley and ſummerſa-

vory, falt and pepper fufficiently ; half a
pound butter worked into four fpoons flour,
to be ftirred in while hot.

Soup, of Lamb's head and pluck.

Put the head, heart and lights, with one
pound pork into five quarts water ; after
boiling one hour add the liver, continue
boiling half an hour more, which will be
fufficient : potatoes, carrots, onions, parfley, fummerfavory and fweet marjoram,
may be added in the midft of the boiling :
take half a pound butter, work it into one
pound flour, alfo a fmall quantity of fummerfavory, pepper and two eggs, work
the whole well together—drop this in fmall
balls into the foup while hot, it is then fit
for the table.

General Rules to be obferved in Boiling.

The firft neceflary caution is that your
pots and covers are always kept clean—Be
careful that your pot is conftantly boiling,
by this means you may determine with precifion the time neceflary to accomplifh any
difh you may prepare in this way——Put
frefh meat into boiling water, and falt into
cold——Never croud your pot with meat,
but leave fufficient room for a plenty of
water—Allow a quarter of an hour to every pound of meat.

To boil Ham.

This is an important article, and requires

particular attention, in order to render it elegant and grateful. It fhould be boiled in a large quantity of water, and that for a long time, one quarter of an hour for each pound; the rind to be taken off when warm. It is moft palatable when cold, and fhould be fent to the table with eggs, horfe-radifh or muftard.—This affords a fweet repaft at any time of day.

To *boil a Turkey, Fowl or Goofe*.

Poultry boiled by themfelves are generally efteemed beft, and require a large quantity of water; fcum often and they will be of a good colour. A large turkey with forced meat in his craw will require two hours; one without an hour and an half; a large fowl one hour and a quarter; a full grown goofe two hours, if young, one hour and a half—and other fowls in proportion; ferve up with potatoes, beets, mafhed turnips, ftewed oyfters with butter.

F I S H.
To drefs a Bafs.

Seafon high with falt, pepper and cayenne, one flice falt pork, one of bread, one egg, fweet marjoram, fummerfavory and parfley, minced fine and well mixed, one gill wine, four ounces butter; ftuff the bafs—bake in the oven one hour; thin flices of pork laid on the fifh as it goes into the oven; when done pour over diffolved

butter : ferve up with ftewed oyfters, cramberries, boiled onions or potatoes.

The fame method may be obferved with
frefh *Shad, Codfish, Blackfish* and *Salmon*.

To *drefs Sturgeon*.

Clean your fturgeon well, parboil it in a
large quantity of water till it is quite tender, then change the water and boil it till
fufficiently done, then hafh it as you would
beef, adding the ufual articles for feafoning. Some prefer it done in the form of
veal cutlet, which is, by taking flices of
fturgeon, dipping them in the yolks of eggs
well beat, then rolled in flour and fried in
butter.

For *dreffing* CODFISH.

Put the fifh firft into cold water and
wafh it, then hang it over the fire and foak
it fix hours in fcalding water, then fhift it
into clean warm water, and let it fcald for
one hour, it will be much better than to boil.

To broil Shad.

Take a frefh fhad, falt and pepper it
well, broil half an hour; make a fmoke
with fmall chips while broiling, when done
add butter, and wine if agreeable.

Salmon or any kind of frefh fifh may be
prepared in the fame manner.

Chouder.

Take a bafs weighing four pounds, boil
half an hour; take fix flices raw falt pork,

fry them till the lard is nearly extracted, one dozen crackers foaked in cold water five minutes ; put the bafs into the lard, alfo the pieces of pork and crackers, cover clofe, and fry for 20 minutes ; ferve with potatoes, pickles, apple-fauce or mangoes ; garnifh with green parfley.

To keep green Peas till Chriftmas.

Take young peas, fhell them, put them in a cullender to drain, then lay a cloth four or five times double on a table, then fpread them on, dry them very well, and have your bottles ready, fill them, cover them with mutton fuet fat when it is a little foft ; fill the necks almoft to the top, cork them, tie a bladder and a leather over them and fet them in a dry cool place.

P I E S.

Beef-ftake Pie.

Take flices of beef ftake half an inch thick; lay them 3 deep in pafte No. 8, adding falt, pepper and flices of raw onion between each laying, dufting on flour at the fame time, together with a fufficient quantity of butter—add half a pint water; bake one and a half hour. This muft be put in an earthen veffel and covered with a cruft as for a chicken pie.

A Lamb Pie.

Take a fhoulder and cut it into fmall pieces, parboil it till tender, then place it in pafte No. 8, in a deep difh ; add falt, pepper, butter and flour to each laying of lamb, till your difh be full; fill with water, and cover over with pafte ; put in a hot oven, bake one hour and a half.

A Stew Pie.

Take a fhoulder of veal, cut it up, and boil an hour, then add falt and pepper, a fufficient quantity, butter half a pound, add flices raw falt pork, cover the meat with bifcuit dough ; cover clofe and ftew half an hour in three quarts of water only.

A Sea Pie.

Four pound flour, one and a half pound butter rolled in pafte, wet with cold water, line the pot therewith, lay in fplit pigeons one dozen, with flices of pork, falt, pepper, and duft on flour, doing thus till the pot is full of your ingredients expended, add three pints water, cover tight with pafte, and ftew moderately two and half hours.

A Chicken Pie.

Pick and clean fix chickens, (without fcalding) take out their inwards and wafh the birds while whole, then joint the birds, falt and pepper the pieces and inwards.— Roll one inch thick pafte No. 8, and cover a deep difh, and double at the rim or edge of the difh, put thereto a layer of chickens and a layer of thin flices of butter, till the chickens and one and a half pound butter are expended, which cover with a thick pafte; bake one and a half hours.

Or if your oven be poor, parboil the chickens with half a pound of butter, and put the pieces, with the remaining one pound of butter, and half the gravy into the pafte; and while boiling, thicken the refidue of the gravy, and when the pie is drawn, open the cruft, and add the gravy.

Minced Pies. A Foot Pie.

Scald neet's feet, and clean well, (grafs fed are beft) put them into a large veffel of cold water, which change daily during a week, then boil the feet till tender, and take away the bones, when cold, chop fine, to every four pound minced meat— add one pound of beef fuet, and 4 pound apples raw, and a little falt, chop all together very fine, add one quart of wine, two pound of ftoned raifins, one ounce of cinnamon, one ounce mace, and fweeten to your tafte; make ufe of pafte No. 3—bake three quarters of an hour.

Tongue Pie,

One pound neet's tongue, one pound apple, one third of a pound of fugar, one quarter of a pound of butter, one pint of wine, one pound of raifins, or currants, (or half of each) half ounce of cinnamon and mace—bake in pafte No. 1, in proportion to fize.

Minced Pie of Beef.

Four pound boil'd beef, chopped fine and falted ; fix pound of raw apple chopped, alfo, one pound beef fuet, one quart of wine or rich fweet cyder, mace and cinnamon, of each one ounce, two pounds fugar, a nutmeg, two pounds raifins, bake in pafte No. 3, three fourths of an hour.

Obfervations.

All meat pies require a hotter and brifker oven than fruit pies : in good cookeries, all raifins fhould be ftoned.—As people differ in their taftes, they may alter to their wifhes. And as it is difficult to afcertain with precifion the fmall articles of fpicery ; every one may relifh as they like and fuit their tafte.

Apple Pie.

Stew and ftrain the apples, to every 3 pints, grate the peal cf a frefh lemon, add rofe-water and fugar to your tafte, and bake in pafte No. 3.

Every fpecies of fruit, fuch as peas, plumbs, rafpberries, blackberries, may be only fweetened, without fpice—and bake in pafte No. 3.

Dried Apple Pie.

Take two quarts dried apples, put them into an earthen pot that contains one gal-

lon, fill it with water and set it in a hot o-
ven, adding one handful of cramberries :
after baking one hour fill up the pot again
with water; when done and the apple cold,
ftrain it, and add thereto the juice of three
or four limes, raifins, fugar, orange peel and
cinnamon to your tafte ; lay in pafte
No. 3.

A buttered apple Pie.

Pare, quarter and core tart apples, lay in
pafte No. 3, cover with the fame ; bake
half an hour ; when drawn, gently raife the
top cruft, add fugar, butter, orange peal,
and a fufficient quantity of rofe-water.

Currant Pies.

Take green, full grown currants, and
one third their quantity of fugar and raifins, to every quart of currants, add half a
pint water, proceeding as above.

POTATOE PIE.

Scald one quart milk, grate in four large
potatoes while the milk is hot, when cold
add four eggs well beaten, four ounces butter, fpice and fweeten to your tafte ; lay
in pafte No. 7—bake half an hour.

N. B. A bowl containing two quarts, filled with water, and fet into the oven, will
prevent any articles being fcorched, fuch
as cakes, pies, and the like.

CUSTARDS.

1. One quart milk, fcalded, 6 eggs, 6

oz. fugar, two fpoonfuls rofe water, half a nutmeg—bake.

2. Sweeten a quart of milk, add nutmeg, rofe-water and fix eggs; bake in tea cups or difhes, or boil in water, taking care that it don't boil into the cups.

3. *Boiled Cuftard*—one pint of milk, two ounces of almonds, two fpoons of rofe-water, or orange flower water, fome mace; boil, then ftir in fweetning, when cold add 4 eggs, and lade off into china cups, bake, and ferve up.

Rice Cuftard.

Boil 2 fpoonfuls of ground rice, with a quarter of nutmeg grated in 1 quart milk, when cold add 5 eggs, and 4 oz. fugar, flavor with orange, or rofe-water.

Baked Cuftard.

Four eggs beat and put to one quart cream, fweetened to your tafte, half a nutmeg, and a little cinnamon—bake.

A fick bed Cuftard.

Scald a quart milk, fweeten and falt a little, whip 3 eggs and ftir in, bake on coals in a pewter veffel.

T A R T S.

Apple Tarts.

Stew and ftrain the apples, add cinnamon, rofe-water, wine and fugar to your tafte, lay in pafte, No. 3. fqueeze thereon orange juice—bake gently.

Cramberries.

Stewed, ftrained and fweetened, put into pafte No. 9, add fpices till grateful, and baked gently.

Appricots, muft be neither pared, cut or ftoned, but put in whole, and fugar fifted over them, as above.

Orange or Lemon Tart.

Take 6 large lemons, rub them well in falt, put them into falt and water and let reft 2 days, change them daily in frefh water, 14 days, then cut flices and mince as fine as you can and boil them 2 or 3 hours till tender, then take 6 pippins, pare, quarter and core them, boil in 1 pint fair water till the pippins break, then put the half of the pippins, with all the liquor to the orange or lemon, and add one pound fugar, boil all together one quarter of an hour, put into a gallipot and fqueeze thereto a frefh orange, one fpoon of which, with a fpoon of the pulp of the pippin, laid into a thin royal pafte, laid into fmall fhallow pans or faucers, brufhed with melted butter, and fome fuperfine fugar fifted thereon, with a gentle baking, will be very good.

N. B. Paftry pans, or faucers, muft be buttered lightly before the pafte is laid on. In glafs or China be ufed, have only a top cruft. You can garnifh with cut pafte, like a lemon pudding or ferve on pafte No. 7.

Goofeberry Tart.

Lay clean berries and fift over them fugar, then berries and fugar, till a deep difh be filled, intermingling a handful of raifins, and 1 gill water ; cover with pafte No. 9, and bake fome what more than other tarts.

Grapes, muft be cut in two and ftoned and done like a Goofeberry.

PUDDINGS.

A Rice Pudding.

One quarter of a pound rice, one quarter of an ounce of cinnamon, to a quart of milk (ftirred often to keep from burning) and boil quick, cool and add half a nutmeg, 4 ounces butter, 4 fpoons rofe-water, 8 eggs ; butter or puff pafte a difh and pour the above compofition into it, and bake one and half hour.

No. 2. Boil 6 ounces rice in a quart of milk, on a flow fire till tender, ftir in half pound butter, interim beat 8 eggs, add to the pudding when cold with fugar, falt, rofe-water and fpices to your tafte, adding raifins or currants, bake as No. 1.

No. 3. 8 fpoons rice boiled in 2 quarts milk, when cooled add 8 eggs, 6 ounces butter, wine, fugar and fpices, a fufficient quantity—bake 2 hours.

No. 4. Boil in water half pound ground rice till foft, add 2 quarts milk and fcald, cool and add 8 eggs, 6 ounces butter, 1lb

raifins, falt, cinnamon and a fmall nutmeg, bake 2 hours.

No. 5. *A cheap one.* Half pint rice, 6
ounces fugar, 2 quarts milk, falt, butter, alfpice, put cold into a hot oven, bake 2 and
half hours.

No. 6. Put 6 ounces rice into water, or
milk and water, let it fwell or foak tender,
then boil gently, ftir in a little butter, when
cool ftir in a quart milk, 6 or 8 eggs well
beaten, and add cinnamon, nutmeg, and fugar to your tafte---bake.

N. B. The mode of introducing the ingredients is a material point ; in all cafes
where eggs are mentioned it is underftood
to be well beat, whites and yolks ; and the
fpices, fine and fettled.

A Tafty Indian Pudding.

No. 1. 3 pints fcalded milk, 7 fpoons
fine Indian meal, ftir well together while
hot, let ftand till cooled ; add 4 eggs,
half pound raifins, 4 ounces butter, fpice
and fugar, bake 4 hours.

No. 2. 3 pints fcalded milk to one pint
meal falted ; cool, add 2 eggs, 4 ounces
butter, fugar or molaffes and fpice fufficient :
it will require two and half hours baking.

No. 3. Salt a pint meal, wet with one
quart milk, fweeten and put into a ftrong
cloth, brafs or bell metal veffel, ftone or earthern pot, fecure from wet and boil 12 hours.

A Sunderland Pudding.

Whip 6 eggs, half the whites, take half a nutmeg, one point milk and a little falt 4 fpoons fine flour, oil or butter pans, cups, or bowls---bake in a quick oven one hour. Eat with fweet fauce.

A Whitpot.

Cut half a loaf of bread in flices, pour thereon 2 quarts milk, 6 eggs, rofe-water, nutmeg and ftalf pound of fugar ; put into a difh and cover with pafte, No. 1. bake flow 1 hour.

A Bread Pudding.

One pound foft bread or bifcut foaked in one quart milk, run thro' a fieve or cullender, add 7 eggs, three quarters of a pound fugar, one quarter of a pound butter, nutmeg or cinnamon, one gill rofe-water, one pound ftoned raifons, half pint milk, bake three quarters of an hour, middling oven.

A Flour Pudding.

One quart milk fcalded, add 5 fpoons flour to the milk while hot : when cool add 7 eggs well beaten, 6 ounces fugar, falt, cinnamon, nutmeg, to your tafte, bake one hour, ferve up with fweet fauce.

A boiled Flour Pudding.

One quart milk, 9 eggs, 9 fpoons flour, a a litte falt, put into a ftrong cloth and boiled one and a half hour.

A Cream Almond Pudding.

Boil gently a little mace and half a nutmeg (grated) in a quart cream; when cool, beat 8 eggs, ſtrain and mix with 8 ſpoons flour, one quarter of a pound almonds; ſettled, add one ſpoon roſe-water, and by degrees the cold cream and beat well together; wet a thick cloth and flour it, and pour in the pudding, boil hard one and a half hour, take out, pour over it melted butter and ſugar.

An apple Pudding Dumplin.

Put into paſte, quartered apples, lay in a cloth and boil one hour, ſerve with ſweet ſauce.

Pears, Plumbs, &c.

Are done the ſame way.

Potatoe Pudding.   Boiled.

No. 1. One pound boiled potatoes, half pound ſugar, 4 oz. butter, 1 pint flour, 1 quart milk and 5 eggs.

No. 2. One pound boiled potatoes, maſhed, 4 oz. butter, 1 quart milk, the juice of one lemon and the peal grated, half a pound ſugar, half nutmeg, 7 eggs, 2 ſpoons roſe-water, bake 1 and a half hour.

Apple Pudding.

One pound apple ſifted, half pound ſugar, 9 eggs, one quarter of a pound butter, one quart ſweet milk—one gill roſe-water, a cinnamon, add 2 ruſks ſoaked ſoft

in wine, a green lemon peal grated (if
fweet apples,) add the juice of half a lemon, put on to pafte No. 7. Currants, rai.
fins and citron fome add, but good without them, bake 1 hour.

Carrot Pudding.

A coffee cup full of boiled and ftrained
carrots, 5 eggs, fugar and butter of each 2
oz. cinnamon and rofe water to your tafte,
baked in a deep difh without pafte, 1 hour.

A Crookneck, or Winter Squafh Pudding.

Core, boil and fkin a good fquafh, and
bruize it well; take 6 large apples, pared,
cored, and ftewed tender, mix together;
add 6 or 7 fpoonfuls of dry bread or bifcuit, rendered fine as meal, one pint milk
or cream, 2 fpoons of rofe-water, 2 do.
wine, 5 or 6 eggs beaten and ftrained, nutmeg, falt and fugar to your tafte, one fpoon
flour, beat all fmartly together, bake one
hour.

The above is a good receipt for Pomp-
kins, Potatoes or Yams, adding more moif-
tening or milk and rofe-water, and to the
two latter a few black or Lifbon currants,
or dry whortleberries fcattered in, will
make it better.

Pompkin.

No. 1. One quart ftewed and ftrained,
3 pints milk, fix beaten eggs, fugar, mace,
nutmeg and ginger, laid into pafte No. 7,

or 3, crofs and chequer it, and bake in
diſhes three quarters of an hour.

No. 2. One quart of milk, 1 pint pompkin, 4 eggs, molaſſes, alſpice and ginger
in a cruſt, bake 1 hour.

Orange Pudding.

Put ſixteen yolks with half a pound butter melted, grate in the rinds of two Se-
ville oranges, beat in half pound of fine
ſugar, add two ſpoons orange water, two
of roſe-water, one gill of wine, half pint
cream, two York biſcuit or the crumbs of a
fine loaf, ſoaked in cream, mix all together,
put it into rich puff-paſte, which let be
double round the edges of the diſh ; bake
like a cuſtard.

A Lemon Pudding.

1. Grate the yellow of the peals of three
lemons, then take two whole lemons, roll
under your hand on the table till ſoft, taking care not to burſt them, cut and ſqueeze
them into the grated peals.

2. Take ten ounces ſoft wheat bread,
and put a pint of ſcalded white wine thereto, let ſoak and put to No. 1.

3. Beat four whites and eight yolks, and
put to above, adding three quarters of a
pound of melted butter, (which let be very freſh and good) one pound fine ſugar,
beat all together till thoroughly mixed.

4. Lay paſte No. 7 or 9 on a diſh, place

or faucers, and fill with above compofition.

5. Bake near 1 hour, and when baked ftick on pieces of pafte, to your fancy, bake lightly on a floured paper; garnifh-ed thus, they may be ferved hot or cold.

Orange Pudding.

Three fpoons of ground boiled rice, 9 of melted butter, 9 of wine, 9 eggs, half pound currants, fix ounces fugar, one pint milk, half a nutmeg, juice of one orange, and one orange peel; lay in pafte No. 7. bake one hour.

Marlborough Pudding.

Take 12 fpoons of ftewed apples, 12 of wine, 12 of fugar, 12 of melted butter, and 12 of beaten eggs, a little cream, fpice to your tafte; lay in pafte No. 3, in a deep difh; bake one hour and a quarter.

A Plumb Pudding.

Take half a loaf of bread, on which pour three pints boiling milk, when cold add fix ounces ground rice, mix the bread and rice together, half a pound plumbs, four ounces beef fuet cut fine, one pound cur-rants, eight eggs, half gill rofe water, one gill wine, lemon peel, fugar and nutmeg as may be agreeable.

Plumb Pudding, boiled.

Three pints flour, a little falt, fix eggs, one pound plumbs, half pound beef fuet, half pound fugar, one pint milk; mix the

whole together ; put it into a ſtrong cloth
floured, boil three hours ; ſerve with ſweet
ſauce.   *Quince Pudding.*

Four quinces boiled ſoft and ſtrained,
to which add eight eggs, half pound ſugar,
four ounces butter, three York biſcuit put
into half pint boiling milk, the juice and
peel of one orange ; lay in paſte No. 3,
bake one and a half hour : ſome add raiſins, but good without them : ſerved with
ſweet ſauce.

PASTES.
Puff Paſtes for Tarts.

No. 1. Rub one pound of butter into
two pound of flour, whip 2 whites and add
with cold water ; make into paſte, roll in
ſix or ſeven times one pound of butter,
flouring it each roll.   This is good for any
ſmall thing.

No. 2. Rub ſix pound of butter into
fourteen pound of flour, eight whites of
eggs, add cold water, make a ſtiff paſte.

No. 3. To any quantity of flour, rub in
three fourths of its weight of butter,
(whites of eggs to a peck) rub in one third
or half, and roll in the reſt.

No. 4. Into two quarts flour (ſalted)
and wet ſtiff with cold water roll in, in nine
or ten times one and half pound of butter.

No. 5. One pound flour, three fourths
of a pound of butter, beat well.

No. 6. To one pound of flour rub in one fourth of a pound of butter, wet with three eggs and rolled in a half pound of butter.

A Paſte for Sweet Meats.

No. 7. Rub one third of one pound of butter, and one pound of lard into two pound of flour, wet with four whites well beaten ; water as much as neceſſary : to make a paſte, roll in the reſidue of ſhortning in ten or twelve rollings--bake quick.

No. 8. Rub in one and half pound of ſuet to ſix pounds of flour, and a ſpoon full of ſalt, wet with cream, roll in, in ſix or eight times, two and half pounds of butter—good for a chicken or meat pie.

Royal Paſte.

No. 9. Rub half a pound of butter into one pound of flour, four whites beat to a foam, two ounces of fine ſugar ; roll often, rubbing one third, and rolling two thirds of the butter is beſt ; excellent for tarts.

SYLLABUBS.

To make a fine Syllabub from the Cow.

Sweeten a quart of cyder with double refined ſugar, grate nutmeg into it, then milk your cow into your liquor, when you have thus added what quantity of milk you think proper, pour half a pint or more, in proportion to the quantity of ſyllabub you make, of the ſweeteſt cream you can get all over it.

A *Whipt Syllabub*.

Take two porringers of cream and one of white wine, grate in the ſkin of a lemon, take the whites of three eggs, ſweeten it to your taſte, then whip it with a whiſk, take off the froth as it riſes and put it into your ſyllabub glaſſes or pots, and they are fit for uſe.

To make a fine Cream.

Take a pint of cream, ſweeten it to your pallate, grate a little nutmeg, put in a ſpoon-ful of orange flower water and roſe water, and two ſpoonfuls of wine ; beat up four eggs and two whites, ſtir it all together one way over the fire till it is thick, have cups ready and pour it in.

Lemon Cream.

Take the juice of four large lemons, half a pint of water, a pound of double refined ſugar beaten fine, the whites of ſeven eggs and the yolk of one beaten very well ; mix altogether, ſtrain it, ſet it on a gentle fire, ſtirring it all the while and ſkim it clean, put into it the peal of one lemon, when it is very hot, but not to boil ; take out the le-mon peal and pour it into china diſhes.

Raſpberry Cream.

Take a quart of thick ſweet cream and boil it two or three wallops, then take it off the fire and ſtrain ſome juices of raſpberries into it to your taſte, ſtir it a good while before you put your juice in, that it may be almoſt cold, when you put it to it, and afterwards ſtir it one way for almoſt a quarter of an hour ; then ſweeten it to your taſte and when it is cold you may ſend it up.

Whipt Cream.

Take a quart of cream and the whites of 8 eggs beaten with half a pint of wine ; mix it together and ſweeten it to your taſte with double refined ſugar, you may perfume it (if you pleaſe) with muſk or amber gum tied in a rag and ſteeped a little in the cream, whip it up with a whiſk and a bit of lemon peel tied in the middle of the whiſk, take off the froth with a ſpoon, and put into glaſſes.

A Trifle.

Fill a diſh with biſcuit finely broken, ruſk and ſpiced cake, wet with wine, then pour a good boiled cuſtard (not too thick) over the ruſk, and put a ſyllabub over that ; garniſh with jelly and flowers.

C A K E.

Plumb Cake.

Mix one pound currants, nutmeg, mace and cinnamon one qr. of an ounce each, 12 eggs, one quart milk, and a ſufficient quantity of raiſins, 6 pound of flour, 3 pound of ſugar, 2 pound of butter and 1 pint yeaſt.

Plain Cake.

Nine pound of flour, 3 pound of ſugar,

3 pound of butter, 1 pint emptins, 3 pints milk, 9 eggs, 1 ounce of fpice, 1 gill of rofe-water, 1 gill of wine.

A rich Cake.

Rub 2 pound of butter into 5 pound of flour, add 8 eggs (not much beaten) 1 pint of emptins, 1 pint of wine, kneeded up ftiff like bifcuit, cover well and put by and let rife over night.

To 2 and a half pound raifins, add 1 gill brandy, to foak over night, or if new half an hour in the morning, add them with 1 gill rofe-water and 2 and half pound of loaf fugar, 1 ounce cinnamon, work well and bake as loaf cake, No. 1.

Potatoe Cake.

Boil potatoes, peal and pound them, add yolks of eggs, wine and melted butter, work with flour into pafte, fhape as you pleafe, bake and pour over them melted butter, wine and fugar.

Johny Cake, or Hoe Cake.

Scald 1 pint of milk and put 3 pints of Indian meal, and half pint of flower—bake before the fire. Or fcald with milk two thirds of the Indian meal, or wet two thirds with boiling water, add falt, molaffes and fhortening, work up with cold water pret. ty ftiff, and bake as above.

Indian Slapjack

One quart milk, 1 pint of Indian meal,

4 eggs, 4 fpoons of flour, little falt, beat together, baked on gridles, or fry in a dry pan, or baked in a pan which has been rub'd with fuet, lard or butter.

Loaf Cakes.

No. 1. Rub 6 pound of fugar, 2 pound of Lard, 3 pound of butter into 12 pound of flour, add 18 eggs, 1 quart of milk, 2 ounces of cinnamon, 2 fmall nutmegs, a tea cup of coriander feed, each pounded fine and fifted; add one pint of brandy, half a pint of wine, 6 pound of ftoned raifins, 1 pint of emptins, firft having dried your flour in the oven, dry and roll the fugar fine, rub your fhortning and fugar half an hour, it will render the cake much whiter and lighter, heat the oven with dry wood, for 1 and a half hours, if large pans be ufed, it will then require 2 hours baking, and in proportion for fmaller loaves. To froft it. Whip 6 whites, during the baking, add 3 pound of fifted loaffugar and put on thick, as it comes hot from the oven. Some return the frofted loaf into the oven, it injures and yellows it, if the frofting be put on immediately it does beft without being returned into the oven.

Another.

No. 2. Rub 4 pound of fugar, 3 and a half pound of fhortning, (half butter and half lard) into 9 pound of flour, 1 dozen of eggs, 2 ounces cinnamon, 3 pints of milk, 3 spoonfuls coriander seed, 3 gills of brandy, 1 gill of wine, one pint of emptins, 4 pounds of raisins.

No. 3. Six pound of flour, 3 of sugar, 2 and a half pound of shortning, (half butter, half lard) 6 eggs, 1 nutmeg, 1 ounce of cinnamon and 1 ounce of coriander seed, 1 pint of emptins, 2 gills brandy, 1 quart of milk and 3 pound of raisins.

No. 4. Five pound of flour, 2 pound of butter, 2 and a half pound loaf sugar, 2 and a half pounds of raisins, 15 eggs, 1 pint wine, 1 pint emptins, 1 ounce of cinnamon, 1 gill rose-water, 1 gill brandy— baked like No. 1.

Another *Plain cake.*

No. 5. Two quarts milk, 5 pound of sugar, 3 pound of shortning, warmed hot, add a quart of sweet cyder, this curdle ; add 18 eggs, allspice and orange to your taste, or fennel, carroway or coriander seeds ; put to 18 pounds of flour, 1 quart emptins, and bake well.

Election Cake.

Thirty quarts flour, 10 pound butter, 14 pound sugar, 12 pound raisins, 3 doz eggs, one pint wine, one quart brandy, 4 ounces cinnamon, 4 ounces fine colander seed, 3 ounces ground allspice ; wet the flour with

milk to the confiftence of bread over night,
adding one quart yeaft; the next morning work the butter and fugar together for
half an hour, which will render the cake
much lighter and whiter; when it has rife
light work in every other ingredient except
the plumbs, which work in when going into the oven.

Independence Cake.

Twenty pound flour, 15 pound fugar,
10 pound butter, 4 dozen eggs, one quart
wine, 1 quart brandy, 1 ounce nutmeg,
cinnamon, cloves, mace, of each 3 ounces,
two pound citron, currants and raifins 5
pound each, 1 quart yeaft; when baked,
froft with loaf fugar; drefs with box and
gold leaf.

Buck-wheat Cakes.

One quart buck-wheat flour, 1 pint of
milk or new beer, 3 fpoons molaffes, 4 do.
yeaft, ftir well together, wet the bottom of
the pan with butter or lard, and when the
pan is hot put in the cakes, when done
pour over butter and milk.

Federal Pan Cake.

Take one quart of boulted rye flour, one
quart of boulted Indian meal, mix it well,
and ftir it with a little falt into three pints
milk, to the proper confiftence of pan-
cakes; fry in lard, and ferve up warm.

New Year's Cake.

Take 14 pound flour, to which add one pint milk, and one quart yeaſt, put theſe together over night, and let it lie in the ſponge till morning, 5 pound ſugar and 4 pound butter, diſſolve theſe together, 6 eggs well beat, and carroway ſeed; put the whole together, and when light bake them in cakes, ſimilar to breakfaſt biſcuit, 20 minutes.

Honey Cake.

Six pound flour, 2 pound honey, 1 pound ſugar, 2 ounces cinnamon, 1 ounce ginger, a little orange peel, 2 tea ſpoons pearl-aſh, 6 eggs; diſſolve the pearl-aſh in milk, put the whole together, moiſten with milk if neceſſary, bake 20 minutes.

Tea Cakes.

One pound ſugar, half pound butter, two pound flour, three eggs, one gill yeaſt, a little cinnamon and orange peel; bake fifteen minutes.

Cookies.

One pound ſugar boiled ſlowly in half pint of water, ſcum well and cool, add 1 tea ſpoon pearlaſh, diſſolved in milk, then two and a half pounds of flour, rub in 4 ounces of butter, and two large ſpoons of finely powdered coriander ſeed, wet with above; make rolls half an inch thick and cut to the ſhape you pleaſe; bake fifteen or twenty minutes in a flack oven—good three weeks.

Another *Chriſtmas Cookey*.

To three pound of flour, ſprinkle a tea cup of fine powdered coriander ſeed, rub in one pound of butter, and one and half pound ſugar, diſſolve one tea ſpoonful of pearlaſh in a tea cup of milk, kneed all together well, roll three quarters of an inch thick, and cut or ſtamp into ſhape and ſize you pleaſe, bake ſlowly fifteen or twenty minutes ; tho' hard and dry at firſt, if put in an earthern pot, and dry cellar, or damp room, they will be finer, ſofter and better when ſix months old.

Tea Biſcuit.

Two pound flour, two ſpoons yeaſt in a little warm milk, mix them together, adding one quarter pound melted butter with milk, to make it into a ſtiff paſte ; bake in a quick-oven, in any ſhape you pleaſe.

Wiggs.

Four pound flour, 1 pound butter, 1 pound ſugar, 6 eggs, 1 pint milk, half pint yeaſt ; mix the flour and ſugar with carroway ſeed, melt the butter, and with the milk mix it all together; bake them quick.

Wafers.

One pound flour, quarter pound butter, two eggs beat, one glaſs wine, and nutmeg to make it palatable.

Tumbles.

Three pound flour, two pound ſugar, one pound butter and eight eggs, with a little carroway ſeed ; bake on tins ; add a little milk if the eggs are not ſufﬁcient.

Biſcuit.

One pound flour, two ounces butter, one egg, wet with milk and break while oven is heating, and in the ſame proportion.

Butter Biſcuit.

One pint each milk and emptins, laid into flour, in ſponge ; next morning add one pound butter melted, not hot, and knead into as much flour as will with another pint of warmed milk, be of a ſufﬁcient conſiſtence to make ſoft—ſome melt the butter in the milk.

A cheap ſeed Cake.

Rub one pound ſugar, half an ounce alſpice into four quarts flour, into which pour one pound butter, melted in one pint milk, nine eggs, one gill emptins, (carroway ſeed and currants, or raiſins if you pleaſe) make into two loaves, bake one and half hour.

Queen's Cake.

Whip half pound butter to a cream, add 1 pound ſugar, 10 eggs, one glaſs wine, half gill roſe water and ſpices to your taſte, all worked into one and a quarter pound flour, put into pans, cover with paper, and bake in a quick well heat oven, 12 or 16 minutes.

POUND CAKE.

One pound fugar, one pound butter, one pound flour, ten eggs, rofe water one gill, fpices to your tafte ; watch it well, it will bake in a flow oven in 15 minutes.

Another *(called)* POUND CAKE.

Work three quarters of a pound butter, one pound of good fugar, till very white, whip ten whites to a foam, add the yolks and beat together, add one fpoon rofe water, two of brandy, and put the whole to one and a quarter of a pound flour, if yet too foft add flour and bake flowly.

Soft Cakes in little pans.

One and half pound fugar, half pound butter, rubbed into two pounds flour, add one glafs wine, one do. rofe water, 8 eggs and half a nutmeg.

A light Cake to bake in fmall cups.

Half a pound fugar, half a pound butter, rubbed into two pounds flour, one glafs wine, one do. rofewater, two do. emptins, a nutmeg, cinnamon and currants.

Shrewfbury Cake.

Half pound butter, three quarters of a pound fugar, a little mace, four eggs mixed and beat with your hand, till very light, put the compofition to one pound flour, roll into fmall cakes—bake with a light oven.

N. B. In all cafes where fpices are named, it is fuppofed that they be pounded
fine and fifted ; fugar muft be dried and
rolled fine ; flour, dried in an oven ; eggs
well beat or whipped into a raging foam.

Diet Bread.

One pound fugar, 9 eggs, beat for an
hour, add to 14 ounces flour, fpoonful rofe
water, one do. cinnamon or coriander,
bake quick.

Molaffes Gingerbread,

One table fpoon of cinnamon one fpoonful ginger, fome coriander or alfpice, put
to four tea fpoons pearlafh, diffolved in
half pint of water, four pound flour, one
quart molaffes, 6 ounces butter, (if in fummer rub in the butter, if in winter, warm
the butter and molaffes and pour to the
fpiced flour,) knead well 'till ftiff, the more
the better, the lighter and whiter it will
be ; bake brifk fifteen minutes ; don't
fcorch ; before it is put in, wafh it with
whites and fugar beat together.

Gingerbread Cakes, or butter and fugar
Gingerbread.

No. 1. Three pounds of flour, a grated
nutmeg, two ounces ginger, one pound
fugar, three fmall fpoons pearlafh, diffolved
in milk, one pound butter, four eggs, knead
it ftiff, fhape it to your fancy, bake 15
minutes.

D

Soft Gingerbread baked in pans.

No. 2. Rub two pounds of fugar, one pound of butter, into four pounds of flour, add 8 eggs, one ounce ginger, 1 pint milk, 4 fpoons rofe water, bake as No. 1.

Butter drop do.

No. 3. Rub one quarter of a pound butter, one pound fugar, fprinkled with mace, into one pound and a quarter flour, add four eggs, one glafs rofe water, bake as No. 1.

Gingerbread.

No. 4. One pound fugar, 1 fpoonful ginger, half a nutmeg, half a pint of milk, one tea fpoon of pearlafh, and 6 eggs, 3 pound flour, bake as No. 1.

Gingerbread.

Three pound flour, two pound fugar, one pound butter, one ounce carroway feed, one ounce ginger, nine eggs, one glafs rofe-water, milk fufficient to make it of a proper confiftence.

A Butter Drop.

Four eggs, one pound flour, a quarter of a pound butter, one pound fugar, two fpoons rofe water, a little mace, baked in tin pans.

To make good Bread, with grown flour.

Take 8 quarts flour, 6 ounces butter, 1 pint of the beft yeaft (this article muft be good) 3 tea fpoons pearlafh, diffolved in half pint warm milk, add this to the yeaft, and after working butter into the flour add the yeaft, and work up the whole with milk into ftiff bread, more fo than of other flour ; the oven muft be heat with light dry wood, but not hotter than for other bread. This method, particularly attended to, will demonftrate that good bread may be made with grown flour.

R U S K.—*To make*.

No. 1. Rub in half pound fugar, half pound butter, to four pound flour, add pint milk, pint emptins ; when rifen well, bake in pans ten minutes, faft.

No. 2. One pound fugar, one pound butter, fix eggs, rubbed into 5 pounds flour, one quart emptins and wet with milk, fufficient to bake, as above.

No. 3. One pound fugar one pound butter rubbed into 6 or 8 pounds of flour, 12 eggs, one pint emptins, wet foft with milk, and bake.

No. 4. P. C. rufk. Put fifteen eggs to 4 pounds flour and make into large bifcuit ; and bake double, or one top of another.

No. 5. One pint milk, one pint emptins, to be laid over night in fpunge, in morning, melt three quarters of a pound butter, one pound fugar, in another pint of milk, add luke warm, and beat till it rife well.

No. 6. Three quarters of a pound but-

ter, one pound fugar, 12 eggs, one quart
milk, put as much flour as they will wet,
a fpoon of cinnamon, gill emptins, let it
ftand till very puffy or light; roll into
fmall cakes and let it ftand on oiled tins
while the oven is heating, bake fifteen
minutes in a quick oven, then wafh the
top with fugar and whites, while hot.

PRESERVES.

For preferving Quinces.

Take a peck of quinces, pare them, take
out the core with a fharp knife, if you wifh
to have them whole; boil parings and cores
with two pounds froft grapes, in 3 quarts
water, boil the liquor an hour and an half
or till it is thick, ftrain it through a coarfe
hair fievc, add one and a quarter pound
fugar to every pound of quince ; put the
fugar into the firrup, fcald and fkim it till
it is clear, put the quinces into the firrup,
cut up 2 oranges and mix with the quince,
hang them over a gentle fire for five hours,
then put them in a ftone pot for ufe, fet
them in a dry cool place.

For preferving Quinces in Loaf Sugar.

Take a peck of quinces, put them into
a kettle of cold water, hang them over the
fire, boil them till they are foft, then take
them out with a fork, when cold, pair them,
quarter or half them, if you like ; take their
weight of loaf fugar, put into a bell-metal

kettle or fauce pan, with 1 quart of water, fcald and fkim it till it is very clear, then put in your quinces, let them boil in the firrup for half an hour, add oranges as before if you like, then put them in ftone pots for ufe.

For *preferving Strawberries*.

Take two quarts of ftrawberries, fqueeze them through a cloth, add half a pint of water and two pound of fugar, put it into a fauce pan, fcald and fkim it, take two pound of ftrawberries with ftems on, fet your fauce pan on a chaffing difh, put as many ftrawberries into the difh as you can with the ftems up without bruifing them, let them boil for about ten minutes, then take them out gently with a fork and put them into a ftone pot for ufe ; when you have done the whole turn the firrup into the pot, when hot ; fet them in a cool place for ufe.

Currants and *Cherries* may be done in the fame way, by adding a little more fugar.

The American Citron.

Take the whole of a large watermellon (feeds excepted) not too ripe, cut it into fmall pieces, take two pound of loaf fugar, one pint of water, put it all into a kettle, let it boil gently for two hours, then put it into pots for ufe.

To keep White Bullace, Pears, Plumbs, or Damfons, &c. for tarts or pies.

Gather them when full grown, and juſt as they begin to turn, pick all the largeſt out, ſave about two thirds of the fruit, to the other third put as much water as you think will cover them, boil and ſkim them ; when the fruit is boiled very ſoft, ſtrain it through a coarſe hair ſieve ; and to every quart of this liquor put a pound and a half of ſugar, boil it, and ſkim it very well ;— then throw in your fruit, juſt give them a ſcald ; take them off the fire, and when cold, put them into bottles with wide mouths, pour your ſirrup over them, cover with a piece of white paper.

To make Marmalade.

To two pounds of quinces put one and a half pound of ſugar and a pint of ſpring-water ; then put them over the fire, and boil them till they are tender ; then take them up and bruiſe them ; then put them into the liquor, let it boil three quarters of an hour, and then put it into your pots or ſaucers.

To preſerve Mulberries whole.

Set ſome mulberries over the fire in a ſkillet or preſerving pan ; draw from them a pint of juice when it is ſtrained ; then take three pounds of ſugar beaten very fine, wet the ſugar with the pint of juice, boil up your fugar and fkim it, put in two pounds of ripe mulberries, and let them ftand in the firrup till they are thoroughly warm, then fet them on the fire, and let them boil very gently ; do them but half enough, fo put them by in the firrup till next day, then boil them gently again, when the firrup is pretty thin and will tard in round drops, when it is cold they are done enough, fo put all into a gallipot for ufe.

To preferve Goofberries, Damfons or Plumbs.

Gather them when dry, full grown, and not ripe ; pick them one by one, put them into glafs bottles that are very clean and dry, and cork them clofe with new corks : then put a kettle of water on the fire, and put in the bottles with care ; wet not the corks, but let the water come up to the necks ; make a gentle fire till they are a little codled and turn white ; do not take them up till cold, then pitch the corks all over, or wax them clofe and thick ; then fet them in a cool dry cellar.

To preferve PEACHES.

Put your peaches in boiling water, juft give them a fcald, but don't let them boil, take them out, and put them in cold water, then dry them in a fieve, and put them in long wide mouthed bottles : to half a dozen peaches take a quarter of a pound of fugar—clarify it, pour it over your peaches,

and fill the bottles with brandy, ſtop them
cloſe, and keep them in a cloſe place.

To preſerve Apricots.

Take your apricots and pare them, then
ſtone what you can whole ; give them a
light boiling in a pint of water, or according to your quantity of fruit ; then take
the weight of your apricots in ſugar, and
take the liquor which you boil them in and
your ſugar, and boil it till it comes to a
ſirrup, and give them a light boiling, taking off the ſcum as it riſes ; when the ſirrup jellies, it is enough ; then take up the
apricots, and cover them with the jelly,
and put cut paper over them, and lay them
down when cold. Or, take your plumbs
before they have ſtones in them, which you
may know by putting a pin thro' them, then
codle them in many waters, till they are
as green as graſs ; peal them and codle
them again ; you muſt take the weight of
them in ſugar and make a ſirrup ; put to
your ſugar a pint of water ; then put them
in, ſet them on the fire to boil ſlowly, till
they be clear, ſkimming them often, and
they will be very green. Put them up in
glaſſes and keep them for uſe.

To preſerve Cherries.

Take two pounds of cherries, one pound
and a half of ſugar, half a pint of fair water, melt ſome ſugar in it ; when it is melted, put in your other ſugar and your cher-

ries ; then boil them foftly, till all the fu_
gar be melted ; then boil them faft, and
fkim them ; take them off two or three
times and fhake them, and put them on a-
gain, and let them boil faft ; and when
they are of a good colour, and the firrup
will ftand, they are boiled enough.

To preferve Rafpberries.

Chufe rafpberries that are not too ripe,
and take the weight of them in fugar, wet
your fugar with a little water, and put in
your berries, and let them boil foftly ;—
take heed of breaking them ; when they
are clear, take them up, and boil the firrup
till it be thick enough, then put them in a-
gain ; and when they are cold, put them
up in glaffes.

To preferve CURRANTS.

Take the weight of the currants in fugar, pick out the feeds ; take to a pound
of fugar, half a pint of water, let it melt ;
then put in your currants and let them do
very leifurely, fkim them and take them
up, let the firrup boil ; then put them on
again ; and when they are clear, and the
firrup thick enough, take them off ;—and
when they are cold, put them up in glaffes.

To preferve PLUMBS.

Take your plumbs before they have ftones
in them, which you may know by putting
a pin through them, then codle them in
many waters till they are as green as grafs,

peel them and codle them again ; you
muſt take the weight of them in ſugar, a
pint of water, then put them in, ſet them
on the fire, to boil ſlowly till they be clear,
ſkiming them often, and they will be very
green ; put them up in glaſſes and keep
them for uſe.

Strawberry Preserve.

Take 3 pound of large fair ſtrawberries,
free from ſtems or hulls, 4 pound ſugar, 1
pound raiſins, place theſe in an earthen pot,
firſt a ſprinkling of ſugar, then a laying of
ſtrawberries, another of raiſins, and ſo alternately till the whole are placed in the
pot, ſet it away in a cool place ; if the
weather ſhould be very warm, frequently
ſprinkle ſugar upon them, by which they
will be preſerved freſh and good.

Apple Preserve.

Take half a peck of large ruſſet ſweet-
ing otherwiſe a fair ſweet apple, pare and
core them ; take 2 quarts of froſt grapes,
boil them in 1 pint water till ſoft, ſqueeze
out the juice, add to this the juice of one
quart currants well ſqueezed ; to this add
3 pound ſugar, alſo 4 whites of eggs, and
the ſhells beat fine, ſcald and ſcum clean,
then add one pint brandy, ſtrain it thro’ a
piece of flannel, then add the apples, and
one freſh orange cut fine ; boil gently half
an hour over a moderate fire, put them in

a ſtone or earthen jar, ſet in a cool place, and keep for uſe.

Damſon Preſerve.

Take 4 pound of ſugar and 1 quart of water, boil and ſcum clean, then run thro' a jelly bag, to which add one freſh orange cut fine, and half pint of brandy; to this ſyrrup put the damſons, let them do over a gentle fire 15 minutes; put away for uſe.

Cherries and *Grapes* may be preſerved in the ſame way.

A new method of keeping Apples freſh and good, thro' the winter and into the ſummer.

Take a quantity of pippins, or other good winter apples; take them from the tree carefully when ripe, and before froſt, make a hole through each one with a gooſe-quil from ſtem to eye, fill this with ſugar, lay them on a linen cloth in a chamber, let them lay in this poſition two weeks, till they are a little wilted, then put them in a tight caſk, and keep them from freezing.

To preſerve buſh Beans freſh and good, till winter.

Take half a buſhel of beans, of a ſuitable ſize and age for eating green, ſtring and break them, then put them into a caſk, firſt ſprinkling in ſalt, then a laying of beans, and ſo alternately till the caſk is full, then add a weak brine ſo as to cover them; take out for uſe, and freſhen twenty-four hours in water, often changing it; boil three hours in freſh water.

To preserve Parsley fresh & green, to garnish viands in winter.

Put any quantity of green parsley into a strong pickle of salt and water boiling hot, and keep for use.

To keep Damsons.

Take damsons when they are first ripe, pick them off carefully, wipe them clean, put them into snuff bottles, stop them up tight so that no air can get to them, nor water ; put nothing into the bottles but plumbs ; put the bottles into cold water, hang them over the fire, let them heat slowly, let the water boil slowly, for half an hour, when the water is cold take out the bottles, set the bottles into a cold place, they will keep twelve months if the bottles are stopped tight, so as no air nor water can get to them. They will not keep long after the bottles are opened ; the plumbs must be hard.

Currant Jelly.

Having stripped the currants from the stalks, put them in a stone jar, stop it close, set it in a kettle of boiling water, half way the jar, let it boil half an hour, take it out and strain the juice through a coarse hair sieve, to a pint of juice put a pound of sugar, set it over a quick fire in a preserving pan or bell metal skillet, keep stirring it all the time till the sugar be melted, then skim the skum off as fast as it rises. When the jelly is very clear and fine, pour it into

earthen or China cups, when cold cut white
papers juft the bignefs of the pot and lay on
the jelly, dip thofe papers in brandy, then
cover the top of the pot and prick it full of
holes, fet it in a dry place ; you may put
fome into glaffes for prefent ufe.

To preferve PLUMBS *and* CHERRIES *fix months or a year, re-
taining all that bloom and agreeable flavor, during the whole
of that period, of which they are poffeffed when taken from
the tree.*

Take any quantity of plumbs or cherries a little before they are fully ripe, with
the ftems on ; take them directly from the
tree, when perfectly dry, and with the
greateft care, fo that they are not in the
leaft bruifed—put them with great care
into a large ftone jug, which muft be dry,
fill it full, and immediately make it proof
againft air and water, then fink it in the
bottom of a living fpring of water, there
let it remain for a year if you like; and
when opened they will exhibit every beau-
ty and charm, both as to the appearance
and tafte, as when taken from the tree.

PEACH PRESERVE.

Take half a peck of clingftone peaches,
wipe them with a flannel cloth, put them
into an earthen pot fufficient to contain
them, fill it up with brandy, let them ftand
two days covered, then pour off the brandy, to which add half a pint of the fame
liquor and four pound fugar ; cut two o-
ranges very fine, which add to the firrup,

and when boiling hot pour over the peaches : the next day fet them into a hot oven, let them ftand half an hour, then fet them away in a cool place. If the weather fhould be warm, the firrup muft be fcalded again in fix or eight days, adding thereto another half pint of brandy and one pound fugar, pouring it boiling hot upon the peaches, then fet them again in a cool place : This method of procedure will give them a more frefh and agreeable flavor, than any mode yet difcovered.

Pears, taking out the feeds, may be preferved in the fame manner.

To dry Peaches.

Take the faireft and ripeft peaches, pare them into fair water ; take their weight in double refined fugar ; of one half make a very thin firrup ; then put in your peaches, boiling them till they look clear, then fplit and ftone them, boil them till they are very tender, lay them a draining, take the other half of the fugar, and boil it almoft to a candy ; then put in your peaches and let them lie all night, then lay them on a glafs, and fet them in a ftove, till they are dry ; if they are fugared too much, wipe them with a wet cloth a little ; let the firft firrup be very thin, a quart of water to a pound of fugar.

To pickle or make Mangoes of Melons.

Take green melons, as many as you

pleafe, and make a brine ftrong enough
to bear an egg ; then pour it boiling hot
on the melons, keeping them down under
the brine ; let them ftand five or fix days ;
then take them out, flit them down on one
fide, take out all the feeds, fcrape them
well in the infide, and wafh them clean
with cold water ; then take a clove of a
garlic, a little ginger and nutmeg fliced,
and a little whole pepper ; put all thefe
proportionably into the melons, filling
them up with muftard feeds ; then lay
them in an earthen pot with the flit upwards, and take one part of muftard and
two parts of vinegar enough to cover them,
pouring it upon them fcalding hot, and
keep them clofe ftopped.

To pickle Barberries.

Take of white vinegar and water, of each
an equal quantity ; to every quart of this
liquor, put in half a pound of cheap fugar,
then pick the worft of your barberries and
put into this liquor, and the beft into glaffes ; then boil your pickle with the worft
of your barberries, and fkim it very clean,
boil it till it looks of a fine colour, then let
it ftand to be cold, before you ftrain it ;
then ftrain it through a cloth, wringing it
to get all the colour you can from the barberries ; let it ftand to fettle, then pour it
clear into the glaffes ; in a little of the pickle, boil a little fennel ; when cold, put a

little at the top of the pot or glaſs, and cover it cloſe with a bladder or leather. To every half pound of ſugar, put a quarter of a pound of white ſalt.

To pickle Cucumbers.

Let your cucumbers be ſmall, freſh gathered, and free from ſpots; then make a pickle of ſalt and water, ſtrong enough to bear an egg; boil the pickle and ſkim it well, and then pour it upon your cucumbers, and ſtive them down for twenty four hours; then ſtrain them out into a cullender, and dry them well with a cloth, and take the beſt white wine vinegar—with cloves, ſliced mace, nutmeg, white pepper corns, long pepper, and races of ginger, (as much as you pleaſe) boil them up together, and then clap the cucumbers in, with a few vine leaves, and a little ſalt, and as ſoon as they begin to turn their colour, put them into jars, ſtive them down cloſe, and when cold, tie on a bladder and leather.

For brewing Spruce Beer.

Take four ounces of hops, let them boil half an hour, in one gallon of water, ſtrain the hop water, then add 16 gallons of warm water, two gallons of mollaſſes, eight ounces of eſſence of ſpruce, diſſolved in one quart of water, put it in a clean caſk, then ſhake it well together, add half a pint of emptins, then let it ſtand and work one week, if very warm weather leſs time will do, when it is drawn off to bottle, add one ſpoonful of molaſſes to every bottle.

EMPTINS.

Take a handful of hops and about three quarts of water, let it boil about 15 minutes, then make a thickening as you do for ſtarch, which add when hot; ſtrain the liquor, when cold put a little emptins to work it; it will keep in bottles well corked five or ſix weeks.

INDEX OF RECEIPTS

ABBREVIATED GLOSSARY

Many of the terms that are unfamiliar to the modern reader have been discussed in historical detail elsewhere. Still, here are a few words that might give difficulty.

amber gum: ambergris, the aromatic secretion of the sperm whale, now used only in perfumery.

American Citron: It concerns the watermelon, which came to the Colonies from its native Africa by way of the slave trade. The preserving method is English.

bullace: a wild plum, sometimes cultivated.

caul: an enveloping fatty membrane.

colander seed: coriander seed, surely a simple typo.

currants, as in "Currant Pie": English currants. Dried currants are identifiable in context, but often referred to by her as *Lisbon currants*.

damsons: an exceptionally fine preserving plum, thought to be from Syria — hence its early name *damascene* — long popular in England, now very difficult to find.

do: *ditto*.

emptins: leavings of fermenting ale or barm, replenished from time to time, adding flour, to serve as yeast; effectively, a sort of *sour dough*.

frost grape: a native American grape.

gill (pronounced *jill*): in American cookery commonly understood to have been the equivalent of 4 fluid ounces, or 1/2 cup.

grown flour: milled from wheat so affected by amylase activity that its gluten has lost the properties that enable it to be properly leavened. This was a recurring problem in damp summers, both in England and the Atlantic states, so that her recipe was useful. It is, of course, not proper bread.

heartslet, more properly *harslet* or *haslet:* the offal. She also uses
 inwards, pluck, and *lights,* old English words for the same.

Indian meal, often simply *indian:* cornmeal. Note that
 modern cornmeals are far dryer than those of
 yesteryear, and so should be cut back in proportion.

ketchup: this refers to earlier English-style ketchups of walnuts,
 mushrooms, or oysters. Tomato ketchup had been
 documented by that time, but was not in wide use; indeed,
 tomatoes are not so much as mentioned in the work.

long pepper: in American works, it refers to whole pods of
 cayenne pepper, one of only two mentions of American
 capsicum peppers in the work.

mango: referring to a method of pickling various fleshy fruits
 or vegetables, small melons, bell peppers, etc., fondly
 thought to resemble the stuffed pickled mango from India.

pearl ash, or *pot ash:* effectively a less refined precursor of
 modern baking soda, which may be substituted, the
 various names not being carefully differentiated. Its
 use was to mushroom in the nineteenth century and
 to become the bane of American baking.

pippins: apples, technically from trees grown from seed
 rather than cuttings, but this distinction was not
 always observed.

plumbs: may refer to plums, although the specific variety
 is more often named, but in cakes and puddings it
 refers to raisins.

race: referring to ginger, a root.

slapjack: probably originally a misreading of *flapjack,* both
 forms long antedating 1796.

stive: to tamp down.

tumbles: surely a typo for jumbles, historically a pretzel-
 shaped rich cookie.

yam: that is, properly, sweet potato.

CPSIA information can be obtained at www.ICGtesting.com
Printed in the USA
BVOW08s1942060916

461308BV00001B/6/P